MW01144704

TERRIBLY CHEESY DAD JOKES

TERRIBLY CHEESY DAD JOKES

This edition published in 2020
By SJG Publishing, HP22 6NF, UK

© Susanna Geoghegan Gift Publishing

Author: Michael Powell
Cover design: Milestone Creative
Contents design: Jo Ross, Double Fish Design Ltd

ISBN: 978-1-913004-05-7

Printed in China

INTRODUCTION

Welcome to this much-anticipated collection of dad jokes which is certified 'terribly cheesy' whilst simultaneously being fresher than a toilet roll with the edges folded over or a hotel pillow with a mint on it.

·······

Nearly half of these jokes are in fact brand new, so you can guarantee that you've never seen them in print before. Isn't it reassuring to think that even though dads have been abusing the English language for their sole amusement for centuries, that their rich funky seam of special 'dad cheese' still hasn't been fully mined?

·······

You'll find shaggy dog stories rubbing shoulders with groan-worthy puns and double meanings, plus plenty of one-liners, knock knocks, doctor doctors, 'what-do-you-gets' and 'did-you-hears'.

·······

No furrow has been left unploughed in the quest to curate this unique crop of clumsy knee-slappers to torture everybody's comedic sensibilities and expand the paternalistic repertoire of not-so-funnies.

PLAYING PONG WITH COFFEE INSTEAD OF BEER:

IT'S A MUGS GAME.

What did the drummer call his twin daughters?
Anna one, Anna two!

Did you hear about the chameleon that couldn't change colour?
He had a reptile dysfunction.

If you're being chased by a pack of taxidermists,
do not play dead.

Which one of King Arthur's knights used to run around the table?
Sir Cumference.

I've been happily married for four years – **out of a total of twenty.**

Nature abhors a vacuum, **but not as much as a cat does.**

4

Why don't eggs tell jokes?

They'd crack each other up.

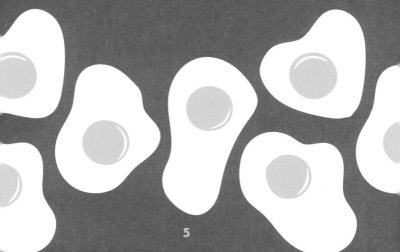

I was climbing a tall conifer tree when I got stuck. My friend went to get help but never came back.
She left me in the larch.

. . . .

Mum: Jimmy, why did you fall in the river in your new school uniform?
Jimmy: I didn't have time to take it off.

. . . .

What did the mouse use to build his house?
Cottage cheese.

. . . .

Which friends should you always take out for dinner?
Your taste buds.

. . . .

Why was the vicar so wrung out after getting caught in a rainstorm?
Because he was a man of the cloth.

Interviewer: Name one of your strengths.
Jobseeker: I fall in love easily.
Interviewer: OK... what are your weaknesses?
Jobseeker: Those big blue eyes of yours.

. . . .

What happens if you eat a duck without plucking it first?
You get down in the mouth.

. . . .

A woman knocked on my door and asked for a small donation for a local swimming pool.
So I gave her a glass of water.

. . . .

I hate bread dough. It's so competitive.
Always having to prove itself.

I built a scarecrow in my shed but it was so heavy that I couldn't even lift it.
I tried everything but I was just grasping at straws.

. . . .

Wife: Just look at that lovely couple down the road, how happy they are. He keeps holding her hand, kissing her, gazing into her eyes. Why can't you do that?
Husband: Are you mad? I barely know the woman!

. . . .

So I went to the rumour mill.
I wove a tapestry of lies.

. . . .

Did you hear about the wooden car with wooden wheels, wooden windows and a wooden engine?

It wooden start.

You can sex an ant by putting it in a bowl of water.
If it sinks, girl ant; if it floats, buoyant.

. . . .

Did you hear about the new restaurant called Karma that just opened?

There's no menu – you get what you deserve.

. . . .

First impressions are rarely correct: most of us have to practise for several hours before we can accurately reproduce someone else's voice and mannerisms.

. . . .

Did you hear about the farmer who ploughed his field with a steamroller?

He was growing mashed potatoes.

I don't hold grudges.
**My mother did and I
hated her for it.**

· · · · · · ·

What do you call a man
who likes to carry things?
Trey.

· · · · · · ·

What do you call a
woman who owns a
particle-beam weapon?
Reagan.

· · · · · · ·

I dislike people with
missing toes.
I'm lack toes intolerant.

The platypus lays eggs
and produces milk,
making it one of the few
animals that can make
its own custard.

· · · · · · ·

What do you get if you
cross a dental hygienist
with a lettuce?
A flossed salad.

· · · · · · ·

You've really got to hand
it to short people.
**Because they usually
can't reach it anyway.**

NO MAN IS AN ISLAND.

TELL THAT TO
ARCHIE PELAGO.

SON: DAD, ARE BUGS GOOD TO EAT?

DAD: LET'S NOT TALK ABOUT THAT AT THE DINNER TABLE, SON.

DAD (AFTER DINNER): OK, NOW WHAT DID YOU WANT TO KNOW ABOUT INSECTS?

SON: AH, IT'S OK DAD. THERE WAS ONE IN YOUR SOUP, BUT YOU SWALLOWED IT.

Never aim for the stars! Always aim just above them, to allow for the effects of gravity, wind resistance, temperature, humidity, etc.

• • • • • • • •

A month ago I sent my hearing aids in for repair. **I've heard nothing since.**

• • • • • • • •

Did you hear about the bashful surgeon who was sacked for gross negligence for causing irreversible blood loss during a routine splenectomy? **And all because she didn't want to gauze a spleen.**

• • • • • • • •

This morning I was mad because I dropped some ice cubes on the floor out of reach, **but now it's all just water under the fridge.**

Pessimist: Things just can't get any worse! **Optimist:** Nah, of course they can!

• • • • • • • •

I tried to swat a fly that was sitting on my garden spade but I think I just made it mad. **It flew off the handle.**

• • • • • • • •

My neighbour bashed on my front door at three o'clock this morning. Can you believe it? **Luckily I was still up playing the drums.**

• • • • • • • •

I attended my uncle's sixty-second birthday party. He said hello, blew out his candles and then **it was time to go home.**

• • • • • • • •

What do you call a sleeping werewolf? **An unaware wolf.**

Why did Napoleon shout at his elbows?
It was his call to arms.

· · · · · · ·

If I ever find the vet who screwed up my limb replacement surgery...
I'll kill him with my bear hands.

Why do dogs sniff each other's behinds?
Because some have a familiar ring to them.

· · · · · · ·

What's the worst thing about throwing a party in space?
Ionizing radiation.

Last Christmas one of my friends gifted me a cute little seabird. She's a really excellent companion, superior to other pets with whom I have briefly shared my life. So this Christmas I intend to reciprocate the kindness by giving my friend a seabird too.
After all: one good tern deserves another.

What do you call an indecisive bee?
A maybe.

What do you call a hen looking at a lettuce?
Chicken Sees a Salad.

What should you do with all your spare umbrellas?

SAVE THEM FOR A RAINY DAY.

What's the most unpopular creature in the ocean?
Public anemone number one.

⋯⋯⋯

Last Christmas I was unable to prepare any of my gifts because my sister stole all the festive tissue paper and sticky tape. At least that's what she said.
Now I can't decide whether she lied or just took the wrap.

⋯⋯⋯

What do you call a Frenchman wearing sandals?
Phillipe Philop.

Did you hear about the vicar who turned his attic into a bedroom with en suite bathroom so that he could have a place to practise his sermons?
He was preaching to the converted.

⋯⋯⋯

My 10-year-old son wants to be the lead singer in an Ultravox tribute band.
But I don't think he's Midge Ure enough.

⋯⋯⋯

What do Kermit the Frog and Attila the Hun have in common?
They both have the same middle name.

TEA-TIME TREAT

I was eating a small, lightly-sweetened cake with lashings of jam and clotted cream but I'm so clumsy I dropped it and could only watch as it rolled underneath the fridge out of reach. I just can't stop thinking about my wayward tea-time treat.

Scone but not forgotten.

I just knew my parents would leave their bodies to medical science.

It was a dead giveaway.

NO MORE HARRY POTTER JOKES YOU SAY?
HAGRID.

I've started investing in stocks, mainly beef, chicken and vegetable.

One day I hope to become a bouillonaire.

. . . .

Don't you hate people who use big words just to make themselves look **perspicacious**?

What did the farmer say when he lost his tractor? **Where's my tractor?**

. . . .

Accordion to a recent survey, inserting musical instruments into sentences largely goes **unnoticed.**

ORNITHOLOGY

An ornithologist was organizing a bird show. Initially, preparations went well, but as the date got closer, one thing eluded her: she couldn't find anyone to adjudicate and award the prizes. Eventually she decided to call her friend who was an expert in shorebirds of relatively compact build with straight bills and large pointed wings. But when her call was connected, all she could hear was birdsong. It appeared that one of her captive shorebirds had answered the phone and was getting increasingly agitated, but her friend was nowhere to be seen or heard. After several minutes of fruitless waiting, the ornithologist slammed the phone down and started crying with frustration. **She should have known that you can't book a judge by its plover.**

NAME A BIRD THAT CAN ROLL BUT CAN'T FLY.

AN EGG.

I BOUGHT A NEW MUZZLE FOR MY PET DUCK THE OTHER DAY.

NOTHING FANCY, BUT IT FITS THE BILL.

Why did the cheetah get disqualified from the race?

He made two false starts.

WHY IS IT BAD LUCK TO FINELY CHOP VEGETABLES WITH THE GRIM REAPER?

IT'S DICING WITH DEATH.

What is black and white, eats bamboo and is very dangerous?

A panda with rabies.

I thought I invented a brand new colour, but it turned out to be a

pigment of my imagination.

. . . .

If the shoe fits, wear it; if it doesn't fit, you've had a lucky escape because who wants to wear **one shoe**?

TERRIBLY CHEESY DAD JOKES

Patient: Doctor, Doctor, I feel like a supermarket.
Doctor: How long have you felt like this?
Patient: Ever since I was Lidl.

· · · · · · · ·

Did you hear about the woman who accidentally booked herself onto an escapology course?
She's really struggling to get out of it.

· · · · · · · ·

A new strain of lice is going around that is resistant to conventional treatments.
It's left scientists scratching their heads.

· · · · · · · ·

I accidentally got locked inside a mirror factory last night.
Still, it gave me time to reflect.

Did you hear about the Japanese animator who hated his boss?
He had manga management issues.

· · · · · · · ·

Did you hear about the invention of garden shears?
It was cutting-hedge technology.

· · · · · · · ·

Liza: Jenny, if you think your boyfriend is handsome, you should see mine.
Jenny: Oh, he's cute too is he?
Liza: No, he's an optician.

· · · · · · · ·

I witnessed a fight between an auctioneer and a hairdresser.
They were going at it hammer and tongs.

What did the carpet say
to the vacuum cleaner?
Eat my dust.

. . . .

A German walks into a bar
and asks for a sherry. The
bartender asks, "Dry?"
The German replies,
"Nein, just the one."

. . . .

What do you call a
Welshman who is
always in debt?
Owen.

It was an emotional
wedding.
**Even the cake was a
gibbering wreck.**

. . . .

What do you call a man
who causes punctures?
Piers.

. . . .

How long does it take to
make all the butter?
An echurnity!

HATS OFF

to all the milliners in the
world because without
them we'd have to invent a
way to acknowledge their
achievements.

Why do melons have weddings? Because they CANTALOUPE.

Driving Ambition

Einstein has to speak at an important conference. On the way there, he tells his driver that they look alike and confesses to him that he's really not in the mood to attend yet another boring conference to give the same old speech. The driver agrees: "You're right. I've watched all of them and I reckon I could take your place and read your notes." So they swap clothes and the driver gives the key note address whilst Einstein relaxes at the back of the auditorium. After he's finished speaking, a cocky young scientist tries to impress the assembled company by asking the great man a really tough question. The driver looks panicked for a moment, before replying: **"That's such a simplistic question, I'm going to invite my driver up here to answer it."**

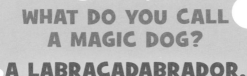

WHAT DO YOU CALL
A MAGIC DOG?
A LABRACADABRADOR.

HOW CAN YOU DESTROY A LIBRARIAN'S REPUTATION?

START A WHISPERING CAMPAIGN.

Why did the scarecrow from Kraków achieve consensus?
He was a straw Pole.

My friend doesn't like to talk about his dry flaky skin.
He'd rather just sweep it under the carpet.

Why do boxers eat so much bread?
Because they gotta roll with every punch.

Did you hear about the Chinese dumpling soup that got vandalized?
It was an act of wonton destruction.

24

Did you hear about the gullible cow who visited a tannery?

She was easily suede.

HOW DO YOU WAKE UP LADY GAGA?

POKER FACE.

Why did the scarecrow win an award?

Because he was outstanding in his field.

· · · · · · ·

Why do bees hum?

Because they don't know the words.

· · · · · · ·

What do you call a woman who's a bit like a melon?

Melany.

Knock, knock.
Who's there?
FBI.
FBI who?
No, we ask the questions.

· · · · · · ·

What do you call a woman who sounds like a fire engine?

Nina.

· · · · · · ·

I can totally keep secrets.
It's the people I tell them to who can't.

WHAT IS BLACK AND WHITE AND RED ALL OVER?

A ZEBRA WITH HIGH BLOOD PRESSURE.

WHAT DO YOU DO WITH A DEAD CHEMIST?

YOU BARIUM.

I'm addicted to cold turkey.
I keep telling people I'm trying to quit but nobody is taking me seriously.

. . . .

Patient: Doctor, Doctor, my son has swallowed my pen, what should I do?
Doctor: Use a pencil till I get there.

What do you call a man with a lisp who can spot a hinged, sliding or revolving barrier at the entrance to a building?
Theodore.

. . . .

What do you call an island full of Scottish comedians?
Billy Colony.

**WOMAN IN LABOUR:
DOCTOR, DOCTOR,
SHOULDN'T! WOULDN'T!
COULDN'T! DIDN'T! CAN'T!**

DOCTOR: DON'T WORRY,
THOSE ARE JUST
CONTRACTIONS.

Why can't you stop a potato from being a potato?

Because taters gonna tate.

• • • • • • •

A man walks into a bar with a piece of tarmac under his arm and says

"A beer please! And one for the road!"

• • • • • • •

What's the shortest prayer in the world about noodles?

Ramen, Amen.

• • • • • • •

What do you call a man with a jar full of eels' eyes?

Elijah.

• • • • • • •

My friend has built himself a shelf for his premium vodka collection.

Absolut ledge.

An amnesiac walks into a bar and sees a beautiful woman. He approaches her and says,

"So, do I come here often?"

• • • • • • •

What do you call a man who looks like a vacuum cleaner?

Henry.

• • • • • • •

What do you call a man who can't access his local-area network?

Nolan.

• • • • • • •

Why is your nose in the middle of your face?

Because it's the scenter.

• • • • • • •

I saw a sign on the train which said 'Please give this seat to an elderly person'.

So I took it to my nan's house.

Patient: Doctor, Doctor, what can I do? Everyone thinks I'm a liar.

Doctor: I find that very hard to believe!

. . . .

Why did the marshmallow lend the chocolate biscuit money?

Because he was a soft touch.

What is small, round and giggles a lot?

A tickled onion.

. . . .

What do you call a woman who resides in this precise spot?

Olivia.

. . . .

A man tried to sell me a coffin today.

I told him that's the last thing I need.

MY WIFE THREATENED TO LEAVE ME BECAUSE OF MY OBSESSION WITH OPTICAL ILLUSIONS. I TOLD HER,

"WAIT, THIS ISN'T WHAT YOU THINK IT IS!"

I wear a stethoscope so that in a medical emergency I can teach people a valuable lesson about assumptions.

. . . .

Priest #1: With the coming of dawn, the angels urged Lot to take his wife and flee out of the city, but she looked back and became a pillar of salt.
Priest #2: What happened to the flea?

I've named my printer Chick Corea, **because it's always jamming.**

. . . .

What do you call an explorer who draws on your hatchback?
Marco Polo.

. . . .

What do you call a man who keeps rabbits?
Warren.

WHY WAS THE CHEESEMONGER LOPSIDED?

HE ONLY HAD ONE STILTON.

A MAN WALKS INTO A BAR WITH HIS ALLIGATOR AND ASKS:

"DO YOU SERVE INVESTMENT BANKERS HERE?"

THE BARTENDER SAYS:

"YES, OF COURSE WE DO!"

THE MAN SAYS.

"OK, I'LL HAVE A BEER FOR ME AND AN INVESTMENT BANKER FOR MY ALLIGATOR."

I FAILED MY DRIVING TEST THEORY. ONE OF THE QUESTIONS WAS: "WHAT SIGN MIGHT YOU SEE ON A COUNTRY ROAD?" APPARENTLY "PICK YOUR OWN STRAWBERRIES" IS THE WRONG ANSWER.

What did the farmer say as he threw a large root vegetable through the library window?
"There's a turnip for the books."

. . . .

What do you call a popular car-park attendant?
A triffic warden.

Is it possible to be a hipster ironically?

. . . .

I asked the hotel receptionist for a wake-up call this morning. She rang me and shouted,
"You're 53, single, morbidly obese and unemployed. What are you doing with your life?"

What do you call a woman who catches fish?
Annette.

I was in an 80s band called The Prevention.
We were better than The Cure.

. . . .

What do you call a man who is easily riled?
Riley.

Patient: Doctor, Doctor, I'm narcoleptic.
Doctor: Go home and try to sleep it off.

. . . .

What do you call a woman who peels fruit?
Cora.

WHAT DID THE CHEESE SAY TO ITSELF IN THE MIRROR?

HALLOUMI.

Did you hear oxygen went on a date with potassium?

It went OK.

. . . .

I burnt my Hawaiian pizza last night.

I should've put it on aloha setting.

. . . .

What if there were no hypothetical questions?

I just got a new job as a street cleaner!

Turns out there's not much training involved, you just pick stuff up as you go along.

. . . .

The first time I got a universal remote control, I thought to myself, **"This changes everything."**

What does an unimpressed sheep say?

Me-e-e-e-e-h!

Why does Bruce Springsteen need to constantly wipe his nose?

Because it was born to run.

....

Fortune favours the bold but what happens to the **italics**?

....

I got caught stealing a leg of lamb from the supermarket. The security guard asked, "What are you doing with that?" I replied, **"Potatoes, parsnips, peas and gravy."**

....

Where are all the laxatives kept?

In the suppository repository.

....

What's so special about the cat's pyjamas?

I was planning to holiday in Norway this year, **but in the end I couldn't af-fjord it.**

....

What did the mother hamster say to the stubborn baby hamster at lunchtime?

"You can go play on the wheel just as soon as you've finished your cheeks."

....

A man walks into a bar owned by horses. The bartender says, **"Why the short face?"**

....

Patient: Doctor, Doctor, I've got delusions of grandeur.

Doctor: I'm pleased you came to see me.

Patient: Well, of course you are.

I was sitting at home drinking soup in my slippers and I thought to myself...
I really must clean some mugs.

My friend decided to get her cheek tattooed with her favourite character from Star Wars.
You should see the Luke on her face.

MY NEIGHBOUR KEEPS RUNNING ACROSS MY LAWN AND THEN PRETENDS TO GET BLOWN UP BY EXPLOSIVES.

I'M TIRED OF HIS MINE GAMES.

What do you call a woman with sharp elbows?
Jocelyn.

I thought it would be easy to balance a bucket of Tippex on my head.
I stand corrected.

WHY DIDN'T THE CHEESE WANT TO GET SLICED?
IT HAD GRATER PLANS.

I do all the exercises every morning in front of the television: up, down, up, down, up, down.
Then the other eyelid.

· · · · · · ·

What do you call an anteater with a short nose?
A canteater.

· · · · · · ·

I swapped our bed for a trampoline.
My wife hit the roof.

I start a new job in Seoul next month.
I hope it's going to be a good Korea move.

· · · · · · ·

Two conspiracy theorists walk into a bar.
There's no way that was just a coincidence.

· · · · · · ·

What's the hardest part about being a vegan?
Keeping it to yourself.

Did you hear about the man whose wife told him to stop imitating a flamingo?

He had to put his foot down.

I got fired from my new job when I asked my very first customer if they wanted 'smoking' or 'non-smoking'. **Apparently, what I should have offered was 'cremation' or 'burial'.**

· · · · · · · ·

Insomniac: Doctor, Doctor, I snore so loudly I keep myself awake.

Doctor: Have you tried sleeping in another room?

· · · · · · · ·

Why can the soft layer of material inside a shoe make blisters worse? **It's adding insole to injury.**

· · · · · · · ·

What is heavy to hold but harder still to drop? **A grudge.**

Did you hear about the bird of prey we bought that only dances to 80s music at night? **Our kestrel manoeuvres in the dark.**

· · · · · · · ·

The teacher gave me a pen, a ruler and a piece of paper and asked me to join A and B by the shortest route. **I really didn't want to, so I had to draw the line.**

· · · · · · · ·

A neutron walks into a bar and orders a drink. The neutron asks, "Bartender, how much do I owe you?" The bartender replies, **"You're a neutron, so no charge."**

· · · · · · · ·

I'm so good at sleeping, **I can do it with my eyes closed.**

Did you hear about the man who put on a clean pair of socks every day of the week?
By Friday he could hardly get his shoes on.

. . . .

Fortune teller #1: We're going to have a hot summer again.
Fortune teller #2: Yes, it reminds me of the summer of 2085.

A bartender says, "We don't serve time travellers in here."
A time traveller walks into a bar.

. . . .

Patient: Doctor, Doctor, can you teach me to do the splits?
Doctor: Well, how flexible are you?
Patient: I can't make Tuesdays.

HOW CAN YOU TELL IF AN ELEPHANT HAS USED YOUR BATHROOM?

BECAUSE OF THE BROKEN TOILET SEAT.

Just had my car waxed. **No idea how it gets so hairy.**

. . . .

I was walking in the park when someone threw a can of cola at my head. **Luckily it was a soft drink.**

. . . .

Patient: Doctor, Doctor, I can talk to the animals.
Doctor: Who gave you my name?
Patient: A little bird told me.

I just drew a terrible self-portrait, **which is very unlike me.**

. . . .

I'm just thrilled with the way the bariatric surgeon wired up my jaw. Food? **I really couldn't ask for more.**

. . . .

A man walks into a bar carrying jump leads. The bartender says, **"Hey buddy, don't start anything in here."**

WHICH CHEESE DO CYCLISTS CARRY WITH THEM?

PANEER.

**PATIENT: DOCTOR, DOCTOR,
I KEEP THINKING
I'M A CHICKEN.**

**DOCTOR: HOW LONG HAVE
YOU FELT LIKE THIS?**

**PATIENT: EVER SINCE
I WAS AN EGG.**

How do you speed up a tardy octopus?
Tell it to shake a leg, shake a leg, shake a leg, shake a leg, shake a leg, shake a leg, shake a leg, shake a leg.

• • • • • • •

I've never been able to count to ten in French because of my **huit allergy.**

• • • • • • •

Patient: Doctor, Doctor, I'm so nihilistic.
Doctor: And why does it **concern you?**
Patient: It doesn't really.

• • • • • • •

What did the car say to its tyres?
Thanks for keeping it wheel.

• • • • • • •

What's the best way to climb onto a frog?
First find a toadhold.

While most puns make me feel numb, **maths puns make me feel number.**

• • • • • • •

I just broke up with my girlfriend Ruth by text.
I'm ruthless.

• • • • • • •

Two vampires on a dinner date:
Vampire#1: So what brings you to this neck in the woods?
Vampire#2: I fancied a bite and heard the food is to die for.

• • • • • • •

Give a man a duck and he'll eat for a day.
Teach a man to duck and he'll never walk into a bar.

• • • • • • •

My apathy causes me heaps of problems, **but I really don't care.**

Boy at disco: Wow, what's a cute girl like you doing in the corner all alone?

Girl at disco: I needed to fart.

. . . .

Did you hear about the surgeon who quit her job at the trepanning clinic?

She was fed up with the hole business.

I can't believe that so many years after the sitcom ended, people are still making Friends references! **No one told me life was gonna be this way.**

. . . .

What do you call a woman who is good at chewing?

Nora.

MAYBE THIS IS THE
BEER TALKING,
BUT I'M AN ALCOHOLIC DRINK MADE FROM YEAST-FERMENTED MALT FLAVOURED WITH HOPS.

WHAT IS A LION'S FAVOURITE CHEESE?

ROARQUEFORT.

Patient: Doctor, Doctor, I can't stop talking about eggs.
Doctor: Are you sure?
Patient: As sure as eggs is eggs.

· · · · · · · ·

Customer: Why is that cake more expensive than all the rest?
Baker: Oh, that's Madeira cake.

I caught my wife going through the neighbour's bins. **She's not nosey, just terrible at parking.**

· · · · · · · ·

My wife is a spokesperson but I'm more of a **hubcap man myself.**

· · · · · · · ·

It takes guts to be an organ donor.

Where do you learn to make ice cream?

Sundae school.

Why are octopi such
rubbish dancers?
**Because they have four
left feet.**

. . . .

Why did the Belgian keep
mixing up his indefinite
articles?
Because he was an twerp.

. . . .

What do you call a man
who wants to be a
US marine?
Jared.

. . . .

I had a dispute with my
neighbour, so to make
amends I took him
round a pot of strongly
flavoured meat stew with
okra, celery, bell peppers
and onions.
Gumbo diplomacy.

. . . .

What do you call a
woman with a badly
attached auditory organ?
Lucia.

Some people say I have a
short attention span, but
– squirrel!

. . . .

I never book tables
at restaurants because
the instant I do
I have reservations.

. . . .

Why couldn't the
sesame seed leave the
poker table?
Because he was on a roll.

. . . .

Why should you only
drink Tequila during
the day?
**Because it's risky to take
a shot in the dark.**

. . . .

Patient: Doctor, Doctor,
I keep thinking I'm a pig.
Doctor: I'm referring you
to a specialist butcher.
Patient: Why?
Doctor: I'm not trained
to cure pork.

WHAT DO YOU CALL A MAN WHO KEEPS BIRDS?
AVERY.

Patient: Doctor, Doctor, can you give me some exercise suggestions?
Doctor: Why don't you try lunges?
Patient: That's a big step.

....

What's the difference between a hippo and a zippo?
One is really heavy and the other is a little lighter.

Did you hear about the cow that lay down on a waste disposal unit?
It was udder destruction.

....

What do you get if you cross a lake with a lifeguard?
Safely to the other side.

....

What's purple, 5,000 miles long and full of pips?
The grape wall of China.

WHICH CHEESE IS MADE BACKWARDS?

EDAM.

Patient: Doctor, Doctor, I keep stealing furniture and it's getting worse.
Doctor: What makes you say that?
Patient: I just took a seat in the waiting room.

. . . .

What do you call a woman whose snake-like fish has escaped?

Lucille.

I've had such a bad morning. First I got into fight with a guy dressed as Shakespeare, then I almost choked on a German sausage.
It's gone from bard to wurst.

. . . .

I bet there are never any workers' strikes at a stress-ball factory.

**Julius Caesar walks
into a bar and says,
"I'll have a Martinus."
The bartender replies,
"Don't you mean a Martini?"
"Look, buddy," Caesar replies,
"If I wanted a double, I'd have
asked for it!"**

Why did the lemon-drizzle slice go for a stroll in the park?
Because it was a piece of cake.

•••••••

What did Sherlock Holmes say when asked to name his two favourite cheeses?
Emmental and Brie, my dear Watson.

Proud Dad (sobbing loudly): It's always been my dream to walk you down the aisle.
Daughter: Dad, you're so embarrassing. Why do you do this every time we go shopping?

•••••••

What do you call a conflicted pig?
Hambivalent.

A GHOST
WALKS INTO A BAR. THE BARTENDER SAYS, "SORRY, WE DON'T SERVE SPIRITS."

Nobody goes
there anymore,
it's too crowded.

. . . .

Customer: I'd like to
exchange this sweater.
Shop Assistant: Certainly
madam, what's
wrong with it?
Customer: It keeps
picking up static
electricity and giving me
tiny electric shocks.
Shop Assistant: I'm sorry
about that. We'll give you
a replacement free
of charge.

. . . .

What do you call a man
who is easily bored?
Emery.

. . . .

What do you get if you
cross a surfer with a
hairstylist?

A beachcomber.

What do you call a
woman with a lisp who
can see into the future?

Thea.

. . . .

What do you get if
you lock a kangaroo
in your car?
A sunroof.

. . . .

Why are eggs so hard to
find at the supermarket?
They're in eggs aisle.

. . . .

Why did the Swedish
tennis legend keep
missing his train?
**He was Björn on
the wrong side of
the tracks.**

. . . .

What did the brave little
sausage say to the big
bully sausage?
"Do your wurst."

Two chemists walk into a bar. The first chemist says, "I'll have a glass of H_2O." The second chemist says, "I'll have a glass of H_2O too."
The second chemist dies.

. . . .

Why did the rookie circus trainer get the sack for overtraining a sea snail?
He wore out his whelk.

. . . .

What did the fork say to the blunt knife?
"Look sharp."

Why did the vegetarian vampire carry a red crayon?
In case she had to draw blood.

. . . .

I have an irrational fear of speed bumps,
but I'm slowly getting over it.

. . . .

The last thing my grandfather said before he died was "Pints, litres, gallons."
That spoke volumes.

WHAT CHEESE IS LIKE DISGUISING A HORSE?

MARSCAPONE.

WHAT'S THE BEST WAY TO COMMUNICATE WITH A FISH?

DROP IT A LINE.

The two rules for success are:

1. Never tell them everything you know.

. . . .

Did you hear about the old lady who plugged her electric blanket into the toaster?

She kept popping out of bed all night.

. . . .

I told my dad that he should embrace his mistakes. He had tears in his eyes.

Then he hugged my sister and me.

. . . .

What's so special about finely ground pork sausage containing cubes of pork fat?

It's just a load of baloney.

Teacher: Have you heard of Murphy's law?

Pupil: Yeah.

Teacher: What is it?

Pupil: If something can go wrong, it will go wrong.

Teacher: That's right. Have you heard of Cole's law?

Pupil: No, what is it?

Teacher: Thinly sliced cabbage and mayo.

. . . .

If people stopped buying haemorrhoid cream **would the bottom fall out of the market**?

. . . .

I'm fascinated by sleeveless upper-body garments.

You could say I have a vested interest.

. . . .

I'm the humblest person I know.

What's green and has wheels?
Grass, I lied about the wheels.

. . . .

Patient: Doctor, Doctor, I think I'm fluorescent.

Doctor: I'd like to keep you overnight for observation.

I had to quit my job at the shoe recycling factory.
It was sole destroying.

. . . .

Why did the detective subject a bucket of soil to a polygraph test?
He wanted to see how the land lied.

HOW DO YOU ATTACH BREAD WHEELS TO YOUR CAR?

WITH DOUGHNUTS.

WHAT IS CHEESE WITHOUT A CRACKER?

CRACKALACKIN!

Why do birds make good politicians?
They have friends in high places.

·······

Can you put the bins out?
I didn't know they were on fire.

·······

Two strangers walked into a bra.
They became bosom pals.

What's round and sounds like a trumpet?
A crumpet.

·······

I bought my friend an elephant for his room, and when he thanked me
I told him not to mention it.

·······

Of course I should clean my windows.
But privacy is important too.

What do you get if you stand between two llamas?

Llamanated.

TERRIBLY CHEESY DAD JOKES

Man: My parrots are stuck together!
Vet: I'm sorry, I can't help – it's toucan fusing.

·······

I finally did it! I bought a pair of shoes with memory foam insoles. **No more forgetting why I walked into the kitchen.**

·······

What has a hazelnut in every bite?
Squirrel poo.

My friend gave me a castle-shaped calculator for my birthday. **I don't like it much, but still, it's the fort that counts.**

·······

So I was in Hades drinking a delicious bright yellow alcoholic beverage made from eggs, sugar and brandy but I pretended not to like it: **it was the devil's advocaat.**

·······

Pensioner: will rubbing goose fat on my back cure my cold?
Doctor: No, you'll go downhill fast.

·······

How many performance artists does it take to change a light bulb?
I don't know, I left after the interval.

LONG HAIR CUT

Ridley Scott went into a barber shop and said,
"Hi, I'm Ridley Scott and I'd like you to
make my hair longer."

The barber replied, "Certainly sir, we supply hair
extensions of the finest quality. How much longer?"

"About forty-five minutes," replied Ridley Scott.

For a moment the barber looked confused,
then his face lit up.

"Ah, now I understand. You want the Director's Cut."

$f(x)$ walks into a bar.
The bartender says,
"Sorry, we don't cater for functions."

IF YOU ARE ATTACKED
BY A GANG OF
CLOWNS, ALWAYS
GO FOR THE
JUGGLER.

Two arsonists went on a date. They had already been carrying a torch for each other, so they quickly struck up a friendship and got on like **a house on fire.**

I played silent tennis today. It's just like regular tennis, **but without the racket.**

The individual who stole an item of Erwin Schrödinger's luggage has been apprehended. **Police described it as an open and shut case.**

Did you hear about the man with five legs? **His trousers fit him like a glove.**

When I'm bored
I like to call up
Best Western Hotels.
When they answer,
"Hello Best Western"
I shout down
the phone,
"The Man Who Shot
Liberty Valance"
and then hang up.

Patient: Doctor, doctor, I can't control my blodder.

Doctor: Your bladder?

Patient: Yes, that's what I meant. I have errotic bowels.

Doctor: And consonants by the sound of it.

Patient: No, just vowels.

. . . .

I need someone to help me sort out the terrible condensation problem in my kitchen.

Pop round anytime, the kettle's always on.

. . . .

How do you get a hipster to eat a hot dog?

Put it in a man bun.

. . . .

'Put your feet up' has a very different vibe to 'put your hands up'.
Never confuse the two.

I freaked out the electrician by opening the door naked. I couldn't tell what gave him a bigger shock – **the fact that I was naked, or that I got into his house.**

. . . .

A penguin walks into a bar and asks the bartender, "Have you seen my brother?" The bartender replies, **"I don't know. What does he look like?"**

. . . .

Did you hear about the Danish physicist who kicked a large desert animal in the goolies?

He was the Bohr that broke the camel's sac.

. . . .

I've got no problem with genetically modified food. **I've just eaten a lovely leg of salmon.**

66

A Packet of Nuts

A duck walks into a bar and says, "Bartender, do you have any nuts?" The bartender replies, "No, we don't sell nuts," so the duck leaves. The next day the duck returns to the pub and asks, "Bartender, do you have any nuts?" The bartender replies, "No, I told you already, we don't sell nuts." The duck leaves and returns the next day and asks, "Bartender, do you have any nuts?" The bartender replies angrily, "Look, I've already told you three times, we don't sell nuts. If you ask me one more time, I'll nail your beak to the wall, understand?" The duck nods and leaves. The next day the duck walks into the bar and asks, "Bartender, do you have any nails?" "No," replies the bartender. "In that case," replies the duck, "I'll just have a packet of nuts."

I've written a book about reverse psychology. **Please don't buy it.**

. . . .

English teacher: Doctor, Doctor, I keep comparing things with something else.
Doctor: That would be analogy.

. . . .

They all laughed when I vowed that one day I would discover the secret of invisibility. **If only they could see me now.**

I saw a television for sale in a shop window, and the sign said, 'TV going cheap, broken volume knob' and I thought to myself, **"Wow, I can't turn that down."**

. . . .

I went to buy some Dr. Martens boots yesterday. I tried them on and asked the shop assistant what made them so comfortable. She replied **"Air sole." I said, "All right I was only asking!"**

DID YOU HEAR THE CHEESY WEATHER FORECAST?
RAIN WITH LIGHT BRIES!

WHEN MY GIRLFRIEND ANNOUNCED SHE WAS LEAVING ME BECAUSE OF MY OBSESSION WITH THE MONKEES, I THOUGHT SHE WAS JOKING.

THEN I SAW HER FACE.

Did you hear about the new shop that just opened called Moderation?
They have everything in there.

. . . .

What is it called when you slap a contented person who can communicate with the spirits of the dead?
Striking a happy medium.

. . . .

My wife was trying to explain to me that I didn't know what irony meant, **which was ironic because I had just had breakfast.**

. . . .

Did you hear the sad story about the fledgling with diarrhoea?
He hit the ground running.

Why are farmers so happy?
For them every day is a field day.

. . . .

Benjamin Button
Benjamin who?
Benjamin
Who's there?
Knock, knock.

. . . .

Whoever stole my antidepressants,
I hope you're happy now.

. . . .

No matter how high or low you set the thermostat it will always **be room temperature.**

. . . .

Waiter, waiter, could I have some more of these small, sweet tasting onions?
Sorry sir, that's shallot.

Why was Lot's wife so highly regarded?
She was a pillar of the community.

. . . .

Will glass coffins be a success?
Remains to be seen.

. . . .

Do you know what makes me smile?
About 26 facial muscles.

How did Elizabeth Bennet flirt with Mr Darcy?
She told him to go jump in a lake.

. . . .

I refused to believe my road-worker uncle was stealing from his job, but when I went to his house, **all the signs were there.**

My best friend is American and she's very intelligent and well-dressed.

Did I also mention that she's a biscuit. For real. Yep, she sure is one smart cookie.

MY CEILING ISN'T THE BEST IN THE WORLD...

BUT IT'S UP THERE.

Patient: Doctor, Doctor, I have no sense of humour and I don't understand irony.

Doctor: One day we'll both laugh about this.

Patient: Do you really think so?

....

What kind of exercise do lazy people do?

Diddly-squats.

Why do scuba divers fall backwards into the water?

Because if they fell forward they'd still be on the boat.

....

I dropped my torch down the toilet. At first I thought it was a disaster but then I realised it was **just a flash in the pan.**

Yesterday, a clown held the door open for me.

It was such a nice jester!

Daughter: Dad, the man next door has stolen our garden gate!
Dad: Well, don't say anything in case he takes a fence.

. . . .

What do you call a group of pregnant tabloid journalists living in South London experiencing false contractions?
Brixton Hacks.

. . . .

Police have introduced a zero tolerance policy towards graffiti.
The writing is on the wall.

. . . .

I used to date a girl with a lazy eye.
Turns out she was seeing someone else the whole time.

. . . .

What do you call one of Santa's children?
A subordinate clause.

It annoys me when people say age is only a number.
It's clearly a word.

. . . .

What do you get if you cross a thermostat with a large sea duck?
An eider-up-and-down.

. . . .

Did you hear about the cat that drank three bowls of milk?
She set a new lap record.

. . . .

Did you hear about the retired baseball player who opened a pizza restaurant that never ran out of tomato sauce?
He covered all his bases.

. . . .

How many hipsters does it take to screw in a light bulb?
Dude, the light bulb was cooler before it changed.

Genie: What is your first wish?
Steve: I want to be rich.
Genie: Granted. What is your second wish, Rich?
Rich: Er... I want lots of money.

I installed a winch to raise my drinks cabinet a few inches off the ground. **It was well worth the effort because it's lifted my spirits.**

Did you hear about the man who discovered a **bee's nest** in his kettle?

He poured it out but then he had a swarm in a teacup.

This Halloween I handed out German sausages instead of sweets. **It gave everyone the willies.**

My friend entered a pun contest. He entered ten, figuring at least one of them would win, **but no pun in ten did.**

WHAT HOTEL DO MICE STAY IN?
THE STILTON.

Knock, knock.
Who's there?
I eat mop.
I eat mop who?
Gross.

. . . .

Did you hear about the
man who swallowed
his wristwatch?
After passing the time
for several hours,
**he eventually passed
the time.**

I just read a book about
Stockholm syndrome.
It was pretty bad at first,
but by the end I loved it.

. . . .

What do you call a worm
that makes films?
Wriggly Scott.

. . . .

What did the cell say
to his sister when she
stepped on his foot?
Mitosis.

76

Did you hear about the nihilistic owl who took a vow of silence?

He didn't give a hoot.

I bought a harp, but now I'm regretting my decision. **It has far too many strings attached.**

· · · · · · · ·

What is even more rewarding than feeding a dolphin? **Serving your porpoise.**

· · · · · · · ·

My doctor said to refer to my nervous breakdown as an episode. **To be honest, it was more like a season finale.**

· · · · · · · ·

The pharmacist sold me some cut price Viagra but **he drives a hard bargain.**

· · · · · · · ·

People are always telling me to live my dreams but I don't want all my teeth to fall out while I'm sitting naked in an exam I haven't revised for.

My main income comes from selling baked dough and churned cream. **It's my bread and butter.**

· · · · · · · ·

Knock, knock.
Who's there?
I dun op.
I dun op who?
Gross.

· · · · · · · ·

How many Genius Bar reps does it take to change a light bulb? **None. You'll have to replace the whole motherboard.**

· · · · · · · ·

Patient: Doctor, Doctor, you have to help me out!

Doctor: Certainly, which way did you come in?

· · · · · · · ·

I often wonder who Pete is and why we do things for his sake.

A man stands over the coffin of his deceased wife. "She smoked all her life and her star sign was Cancer, so it was a big shock when she was **eaten by a giant crab.**"

. . . .

What do you call a Spanish guy who has been discharged from hospital?
Manuel.

. . . .

After careful consideration of all its pros and cons, I finally bought myself this cool **double-edged sword.**

. . . .

What's the only thing you can catch by slowing down?
Your breath.

. . . .

What do you call a line of Barbies?
A Barbie queue.

I've just discovered that the name Niamh is pronounced 'Neeve'.
Unbeliamhable.

. . . .

A grouse waddles into a bar and the bartender says, "We have a blended Scotch whisky named after you!"
The grouse replies, **"You have a whisky called Colin?"**

How did the bossy man become most popular person in the bar?
He ordered everyone a round.

. . . .

My grandfather spent thirty years working as a lift attendant.
He said it was a great job with more than its fair share of ups and downs.

. . . .

I've started having six sugars in my tea.
It's causing quite a stir.

The pest controller just informed me that the wooden rafters in my attic are infested with fungus.
I want a second opinion because I think he's talking rot.

. . . .

Always remember:
You're just as unique as everybody else.

. . . .

How many freestyle skateboarders does it take to change a light bulb?
One, but it takes him 100 tries.

TALK IS CHEAP BUT BIRDSONG IS CHEEPIER

I WAS ON THE INTERNATIONAL SPACE STATION AND MISLAID MY GRAVITY BOOTS.

I TURNED THE PLACE UPSIDE DOWN LOOKING FOR THEM.

My wife ran off with a tractor salesman. **She left me a John Deere letter.**

• • • • • • •

My husband and I both love cheese triangles but he always eats the last one in the packet and never thinks to offer it to me. **I'm worried it's starting to drive a wedge between us.**

• • • • • • •

Did you know that A A Milne, the creator of Winnie the Pooh, had a smaller brother called **A A A Milne.**

• • • • • • •

Linguistics Professor #1: I just baked some synonym buns.

Linguistics Professor #2: You mean, like the ones grammar used to make?

Did you hear about the surgeon who formed her own organ donor company? **She really put her heart into it.**

• • • • • • •

Did you hear about the joke that didn't have a punch line?

• • • • • • •

I often wonder what it was exactly that the Knights in White sat in?

• • • • • • •

Knock, knock.
Who's there?
Tank.
Tank who?
You're welcome.

• • • • • • •

Which figurative oleaginous unguent increases the harder you polish? **Elbow grease.**

Decent Pockets

Did you hear the heart warming story about the resourceful tailor who lined his own pockets, in his lunch break or after hours? He simply had the skills and the diligence to literally add linings to his own pockets without doing anything else that could be construed as greedy or deceitful. It would be nice if more people were as honest and inventive as him.

. . . .

While my wife was out last week, I decorated our bedroom with a design based on pictures of small dogs.

She was not happy and accused me of having an

all terrier motif.

I BOUGHT A BED FOR
THE SPARE ROOM.
IT'S SOMETHING
TO FALL
BACK ON

Why don't shellfish
give to charity?
**Because they're
exoskeleton-bearing
aquatic invertebrates.**

Knock, knock.
Who's there?
To.
To who?
It's to whom.

Did you hear about the
orienteer with no sense
of direction?
**He packed up his stuff
and right.**

Why should you never
be surprised when you
run out of oak-aged corn
whiskey ?
**It's a Bourbon
conclusion.**

What's the best way to handle a baby goat?

With kid gloves.

I went to the beach today, and decided to throw pebbles at every seabird there.
I left no tern unstoned.

....

Justice is a dish best served cold; if it was served warm it would **be justwater.**

....

Last Halloween I handed out pancakes instead of sweets.
It gave everyone the crêpes.

....

What do you call a flock of baby sheep rolling down the hill?
A lambslide.

....

How do you tell the difference between a crocodile and an alligator?
You will see one later and one in a while.

Why not go out on a limb?
Isn't that where all the fruit is?

....

Did you hear about the cowboy who wore paper clothes?
He was jailed for rustling.

....

Teacher: I thought I told you to stand at the end of the line.
Johnny: I tried but there was already somebody there.

....

Why are airline pilots so easily distracted?
They often have their heads in the clouds.

....

Strong people don't put others down.
They lift them up and slam them on the ground.

Marks out of Ten

I bought some new soft furnishings for the lounge and invited a few friends round to show them off. Everyone was very complementary but Mandy insisted on writing a short appraisal and marking them out of ten.
She's an armchair critic.

What do you get hanging off banana trees?

Sore arms.

What did the violin say to the highly-strung guitar?
Fret not!

Which of King Arthur's knights couldn't remember the year of his birth?
Sir Ca.

Which side of a chicken has the most feathers?
The outside.

Did you hear about the cartoonist found dead at his home?
Details are sketchy.

DID YOU HEAR ABOUT THE INVISIBLE FLOWER?

IT'S NOTHING TO SNIFF AT.

Billy: Daddy, if I show you something, do you promise to keep it under your hat?

Dad: Of course son, cross my heart.

Billy: Look at this dog poo.

. . . .

Live for the moment but **plan for the morning after the night before.**

Knock, knock.
Who's there?
Agad.
Agad who?
Push pineapple shake the tree.

. . . .

I'm not very empathetic, but I have friends who are **so I just imagine how they must feel.**

What do you call a snowman with a six pack?

An abdominal snowman.

Knock, knock.
Who's there?
Interrupting raven.
Interrupt–
CAAWW!!

• • • • • • •

Just before payday
when I'm broke I smear
peanut butter on my
kitchen furniture,
so no matter what,
**I always put food
on the table.**

• • • • • • •

How many cops does
it take to change a
light bulb?
None. It turned itself in.

• • • • • • •

Did you hear about the
industrial lathe operator
who loved his work so
much that he died at
his work station?
**They say he's still
turning in his grave.**

I didn't say it was
your fault,
I said I was blaming you.

• • • • • • •

Knock, knock.
Who's there?
Palin.
Palin who?
Palin comparison.

• • • • • • •

Why did the puma get on
well with other pumas?
**She had a good sense
of puma.**

• • • • • • •

Why do mice always
pass exams?
They squeak through.

• • • • • • •

A truck overturned and
spilled its load of Vicks
vapour rub on
the motorway.
**Amazingly, there was
no congestion for up
to eight hours.**

Did you hear about the guy who invented Tic Tacs?

They say he made a mint.

· · · · · · · ·

Knock, knock.
Who's there?
A chore.
A chore who?
A chore disposal.

· · · · · · · ·

What do you call a cow that just gave birth?

Decalfinated.

Patient: Doctor, Doctor, I'm really lazy and my shins are freezing.

Doctor: It's time you pulled your socks up.

· · · · · · · ·

Knock, knock.
Who's there?
Fergie F.
Fergie F who?
Fergie F me for bothering you.

What's brown and sticky?

Lots of things: warm toffee, mud, melted chocolate, fresh dog poo...

What do you call an alligator in a vest?

An investigator.

....

Knock, knock.
Who's there?
Tuna.
Tuna who?
Tuna avail.

....

Did you hear about the piglets who wanted to do something special for their mother's birthday?

They threw a sowprize party.

How do mathematicians scold their children?

"If I've told you n times, I've told you (n+1) times..."

....

My grandma insists that she lost her hearing when she was in Rome. Whenever I ask her if she's sure, she says, **"Yes, deaf in Italy."**

....

Did you hear about the accident-prone butcher? **He has fingers in lots of pies.**

WHO'S THE COOLEST PERSON IN THE HOSPITAL?

THE ULTRASOUND GUY.

I WENT TO A FANCY DRESS COMPETITION LAST NIGHT DRESSED AS A GIRAFFE.

I DIDN'T WIN BUT AT LEAST I CAN HOLD MY HEAD UP HIGH.

Knock, knock.
Who's there?
HB4.
HB4 who?
HB4 beauty.

....

After dinner my wife asked me if I could clear the table.
I needed a run up, but I made it.

....

Did you hear about the New York mechanic who fell asleep underneath his car?
He woke up really oily.

....

A couple of biologists had twins.
They named one Jessica and the other Control.

....

If you're not part of the solution, you're part of **the precipitate.**

Patient: Doctor, Doctor, I keep thinking I'm a lemon.
Doctor: We'll have to run some zests.

....

What is the correct way to enter a room occupied by one of the wives of Henry VIII?
Just amble in.

....

My hair is so long, it started growing its own hair.
Don't take that too seriously, it's metafollicle.

....

Yesterday John Doe robbed Peter to pay Paul, but they don't know Jack, who owes either Tom, Dick or Harry, so how can we ever hope to be even Stephen?

What do you call an uncivil person who designs and builds machines or structures?

A rude engineer.

. . . .

Before the operation the anaesthetist gave me the choice of being knocked out with gas or a boat paddle.

It was an ether/oar situation.

. . . .

Where there's smoke there's usually an idiot doing doughnuts in a car park to impress his stupid friends.

. . . .

Did you hear about the geologist who attracted criticism for his huge collection of fine-grained, foliated, homogeneous metamorphic rock?

He was slated for it.

Why don't ants get sick?

Because they have little anty bodies.

. . . .

I wouldn't want a monopoly in hot beverages **for all the tea in China.**

. . . .

Life is a bowl of cherries: existential torment rendered momentarily less tedious by the occasional appearance of yoghurt.

I LOVE CHEESY JOKES ABOUT EYES.

THE CORNEA THE BETTER.

If you had ten oranges in one hand and ten pears in the other hand, what would you have?
Massive hands.

....

Waiter, Waiter, there's a hedgehog in my glass.
I'm sorry sir, someone must have spiked your drink.

My friend wrote a newspaper article about seatbelts.
It's a safety feature.

....

What did the disciples eat at the last breakfast?
Corpus Krispies.

....

I can be spontaneous, **if I have plenty of time to prepare.**